SMART CHARTS

OCEANS

By Madeline Tyler

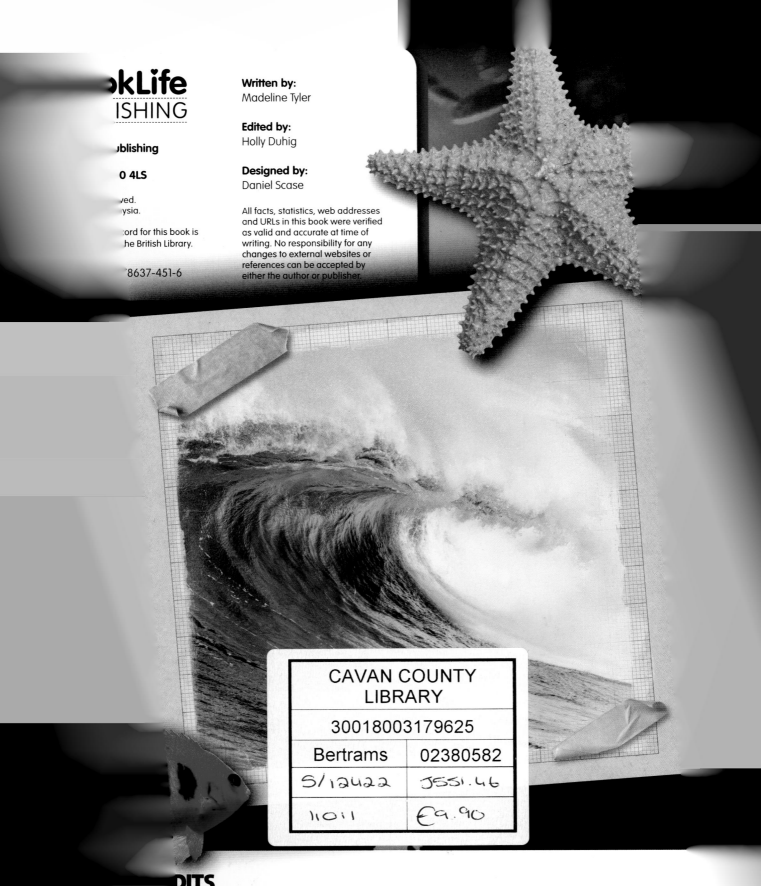

kLife
ISHING

ublishing

0 4LS

ved.
ysia.

ord for this book is
he British Library.

8637-451-6

Written by:
Madeline Tyler

Edited by:
Holly Duhig

Designed by:
Daniel Scase

DITS

e, mexrix, Christian Musat, arka38, EpicStockMedia, Lokichen. 2 – Picsfive, arka38, EpicStockMedia. 3 – Christian Musat, ark ogorelova Olga. 6 – Kitnha, Nechayka. 7 – KnottoSS, Paul S. Wolf. 8 – Brostock, Rainer Lesniewski. 9 – Rich Carey. 10 – Captain an Ledgard. 12 – NASA. 13 – Sky vectors. 14 – Amanita Silvicora, rvika. 15 – PHOTO JUNCTION, Rvector. 16 – Oleg Vyshnevskyy . 17 – Besjunior. 18 – atiger, lassedesignen. 19 – Brian Kinney, bluehand. 20 – Adam Twibell, mapichai. 21 – Lidiya Oleandra, Annable, LuckyVector, Miss Fortuna. 23 –CrystalView, svetabelaya. 24 – corbac40, Sharky11. 25 – rangsan paidaen, mTaira. s Furian, Andrew Koturanov. 28 – urbans. 29 – Jamie Wilson, NordNordWest. 30 – Doremi, robuart. Graph paper throughout: koF. Coral throughout – arka38. Vector coral throughout – Lokichen. Starfish throughout – Kletr. Images are courtesy of o Getty Images, Thinkstock Photo and iStockphoto.

OCEANS

SMART CHARTS

Words that look like **THIS** are explained in the glossary on page 31.

KNOW YOUR CHARTS!

WHAT IS DATA?

Data is another word for information. Data can be facts, numbers, words, measurements or descriptions. For example, someone might collect data about the different types of houses along a street. They might record how many houses there are, what colour they are, and when they were built. Data can be difficult to understand, or INTERPRET, if it's a long list of words and numbers, so people make it easier to read by showing it on a table, chart or graph. Different types of charts and graphs can be used to show different types of data.

TABLES AND TALLY MARKS

HOUSE COLOUR	TALLY	TOTAL
RED	⊬⊬⊬ l	6
BLUE	lll	3
GREEN	ll	2
BROWN	⊬⊬⊬ lll	8
YELLOW	l	1

Tables are used to write down data about different things. They are usually quite simple and have a few rows or columns. Tally marks are used to count things up. The tally marks can be recorded in a frequency table. This shows how many of each thing there are. Tally marks are drawn in sets of five to make them easier to count. You draw four lines and then the fifth one strikes through the others.

PICTOGRAMS

You can use the data from a frequency table to make a pictogram. Pictograms show the same information but with pictures or symbols.

RED	⌂⌂⌂	6
BLUE	⌂⌊	3
GREEN	⌂	2
BROWN	⌂⌂⌂⌂	8
YELLOW	⌊	1
KEY: ⌂ =2		

Bar charts usually show data that can easily be split into different groups, such as colours or months. You can easily compare the data in a bar chart and see which column is the highest.

BAR CHARTS

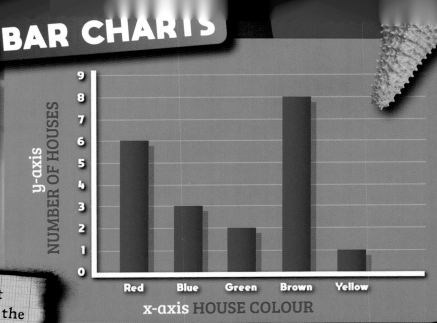

Graphs have two axes. The one that goes up and down is the y-axis and the one that goes left to right is the x-axis.

PIE CHARTS

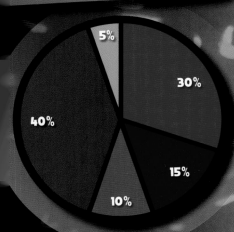

Pie charts are usually circular. They are split into different slices, just like a pie! Pie charts show data compared to the total number of something. For example, the total number of houses on the street is 20. Two of the houses are green – this is ten percent (10%) or one-tenth (1/10).

LINE GRAPHS

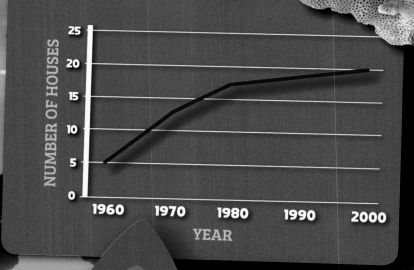

Line graphs show if there is a correlation (a connection or trend) between two sets of data. This line graph shows that there is a **POSITIVE CORRELATION** between the number of houses and time – the number of houses has increased as time has passed.

OCEANS

Oceans are massive bodies of water that can be found all around the world. There are five oceans on Earth and they surround the **CONTINENTS**. The oceans are so large that, of the 71% of Earth that is covered in water, 97% of this water is in the oceans. The other 3% is freshwater that can be found in lakes, rivers and streams, and frozen water that's trapped in **GLACIERS**, and the polar ice caps and ice sheets at the very north and south of the world.

ARCTIC OCEAN

ATLANTIC OCEAN

PACIFIC OCEAN

INDIAN OCEAN

SOUTHERN OCEAN

The Earth's ice sheets can be found in Greenland and Antarctica. As Earth's **CLIMATE** gets warmer, the ice sheets are slowly melting.

WATER   LAND

OCEANS   OTHER WATER

The oceans are very important to life on Earth. They provide **HABITATS** for living things, affect our weather and climate, and produce lots of oxygen that we need to survive. So far, we've only explored around 5% of the world's oceans, so there's lots more to discover and learn about our planet!

PACIFIC OCEAN

There are five oceans: the Pacific Ocean, the Atlantic Ocean, the Indian Ocean, the Arctic Ocean and the Southern Ocean. The largest of these is the Pacific Ocean. It covers over a third of the Earth's surface and separates the Americas from Asia and Australia. Because the Pacific Ocean is so big, its conditions can be very different depending on where you are in the world. In the very north and south, the waters are cold and icy, but near the **EQUATOR** around the middle of the Earth, the water is very warm.

ARCTIC OCEAN

The Arctic Ocean is the world's smallest ocean. It surrounds the Arctic and can also be found along the northern coasts of the US, Canada, Greenland, Scandinavia and Russia. The temperature of the Arctic can range from 0 degrees Celsius (°C) in the summer to -40°C in the winter, when a lot of it is frozen solid.

Some animals, including this humpback whale, migrate from cooler areas of the Pacific in summer to warmer areas in winter. Migration is when animals move to different regions on Earth at different points of the year.

OCEAN LAYERS

The oceans aren't the same depth all over the world. Some parts close to the land are very shallow and other parts farther out in the open ocean are thousands of metres deep. Oceans are usually divided into five layers, or zones. These different zones receive different amounts of sunlight. For example, the epipelagic, or sunlit, zone is very close to the ocean's surface and receives lots of sunlight. However, the deepest part of the ocean – the hadopelagic, or hadal, zone – receives no sunlight at all and is in **CONSTANT** darkness.

200 m	EPIPELAGIC ZONE (SUNLIT ZONE)
1,000 m	MESOPELAGIC ZONE (TWILIGHT ZONE)
2,000 m	
3,000 m	BATHYPELAGIC ZONE (BATHYAL OR MIDNIGHT ZONE)
4,000 m	
5,000 m	ABYSSOPELAGIC ZONE (ABYSSAL ZONE)
6,000 m	
7,000 m	
8,000 m	
9,000 m	
10,000 m	
11,000 m	HADOPELAGIC ZONE (HADAL ZONE)

The hadal zone is made up of huge underwater trenches that stretch for thousands of kilometres (km) across the ocean floor. Most trenches are formed because of tectonic plates. Tectonic plates are the huge sections of rock that make up the Earth's surface, or **CRUST**. When one plate slides beneath, or subducts, another plate, trenches are formed. Many trenches can be found in the Pacific Ocean along the plate boundaries where the Pacific Plate subducts underneath the Australian, North American and Philippine Sea Plates.

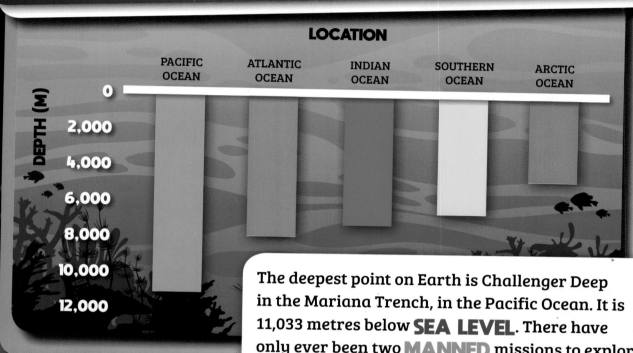

LOCATION

DEPTH (M)

| PACIFIC OCEAN | ATLANTIC OCEAN | INDIAN OCEAN | SOUTHERN OCEAN | ARCTIC OCEAN |

0
2,000
4,000
6,000
8,000
10,000
12,000

This bar chart shows the deepest points in Earth's five oceans.

The deepest point on Earth is Challenger Deep in the Mariana Trench, in the Pacific Ocean. It is 11,033 metres below **SEA LEVEL**. There have only ever been two **MANNED** missions to explore Challenger Deep. The first trip was made by two men, Jacques Piccard and Don Walsh, aboard the ship Trieste in 1960. The second was made in 2012 by the film director James Cameron in a deep-diving submarine called the Deepsea Challenger.

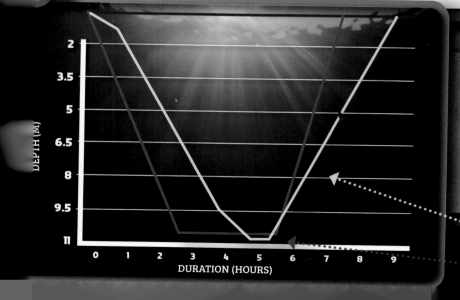

DEPTH (M)

2
3.5
5
6.5
8
9.5
11

DURATION (HOURS)
0 1 2 3 4 5 6 7 8 9

This line graph shows us that, although the Trieste reached slightly deeper than the Deepsea Challenger, the Deepsea Challenger spent much more time in the depths of the trench.

TRIESTE
MAXIMUM DEPTH: 10,916 m

DEEPSEA CHALLENGER
MAXIMUM DEPTH: 10,898 m

MID-ATLANTIC RIDGE

Tectonic plates beneath the ocean don't just create deep trenches. Over millions of years, huge, underwater mountains and volcanos have been formed by tectonic plates slowly moving towards and away from each other. In fact, the longest chain of mountains on Earth is actually underwater at the bottom of the Atlantic Ocean! This mountain range is called the Mid-Atlantic Ridge and it runs for 16,000 km along the floor of the Atlantic Ocean, from Iceland near the Arctic Ocean, to the southern tip of Africa near the Southern Ocean.

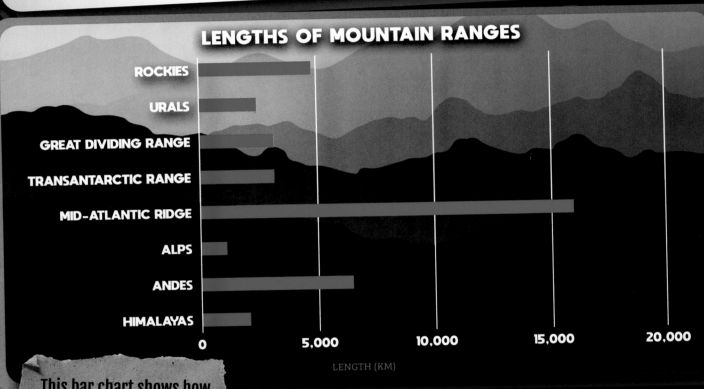

LENGTHS OF MOUNTAIN RANGES

ROCKIES
URALS
GREAT DIVIDING RANGE
TRANSANTARCTIC RANGE
MID-ATLANTIC RIDGE
ALPS
ANDES
HIMALAYAS

0   5,000   10,000   15,000   20,000

LENGTH (KM)

This bar chart shows how long the Mid-Atlantic Ridge is compared to some of the other longest mountain ranges on Earth. It's twice as long as the Andes, which is the longest mountain range on land.

The Mid-Atlantic Ridge lies between the North American and Eurasian plates and the African and South American plates. These plates are moving away from each other, causing the ridge to get wider. As the ridge widens, magma comes up from the Earth's mantle and cools to create mountains, ridges, islands and volcanos.

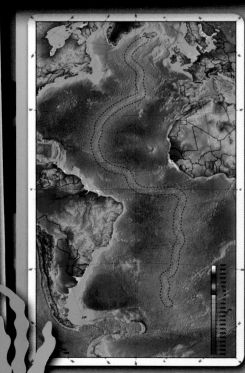

Part of the Mid-Atlantic Ridge can be seen in Iceland's Thingvellir National Park. Tourists can walk along the Thingvellir Rift Valley between the Eurasian and North American plates.

Although most of the Mid-Atlantic Ridge is underwater, around 10% rises above the ocean surface as islands. Nine island regions lie along the Mid-Atlantic Ridge and one of these islands is Iceland. Scientists believe that Iceland was formed millions of years ago when hot magma from the Earth's mantle erupted from the Mid-Atlantic Ridge as lava. The lava then collected and cooled above the ocean surface to eventually form the island of Iceland.

RE IS THE ATLANTIC RIDGE?

- ○ ABOVE SEA
- ● UNDERWATER

The Mid-Atlantic Ridge reaches heights of around 3,000 m above the ocean floor, but most of this is hidden underwater. The highest PEAK in Iceland is Hvannadalshnúkur on the Öræfajökull volcano. It stands at 2,110 m above sea level and is the third-tallest peak along the Mid-Atlantic Ridge after Mount Pico in Azores and Beerenberg in Jan Mayen.

HIGHEST PEAKS OF ISLANDS ALONG THE MID-ATLANTIC RIDGE

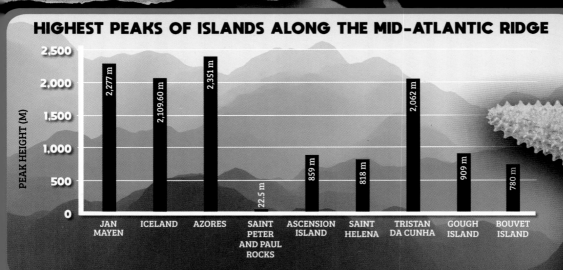

PEAK HEIGHT (M)

JAN MAYEN	2,277 m
ICELAND	2,109.60 m
AZORES	2,351 m
SAINT PETER AND PAUL ROCKS	22.5 m
ASCENSION ISLAND	859 m
SAINT HELENA	818 m
TRISTAN DA CUNHA	2,062 m
GOUGH ISLAND	909 m
BOUVET ISLAND	780 m

SEAS
THE SEVEN SEAS

You may have heard people talk about the 'seven seas' before, but did you know that there are actually far more than seven? No one knows for sure exactly how many seas there are on Earth, but most people agree that the number is somewhere between 70 and 90! Seas are slightly smaller than oceans and are usually closer to land. Some are even completely **LANDLOCKED**!

The largest sea is the Philippine Sea, which lies to the east and northeast of the Philippines in the Pacific Ocean. The Philippine Sea Plate makes up the floor of the Philippine Sea. It's surrounded by plate boundaries which, over millions of years, have created many ocean trenches, including the deepest of them all – the Mariana Trench.

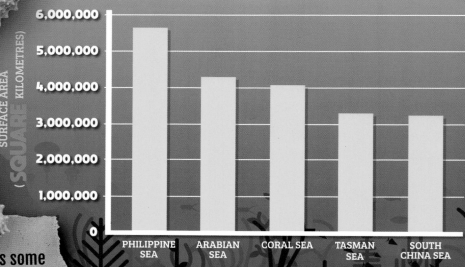

LARGEST SEAS

This bar chart shows some of the world's seas that have the largest surface area. Surface area is how much land something like a lake or a house takes up.

Seawater, which can be found in oceans and seas, is salty. Freshwater isn't salty. Lakes are usually freshwater, but a few are actually saltwater. Some of these lakes are so big and so salty that many people call them 'seas', even though they're completely surrounded by land.

The Caspian Sea is the largest saltwater lake in the world. It lies between Europe and Asia and has **SHORES** in Turkmenistan, Iran, Azerbaijan, Russia and Kazakhstan. The Caspian Sea used to be connected to the rest of the world's seas and oceans until it became landlocked millions of years ago.

DEAD SEA SALINITY

SEAWATER SALINITY

● SALT ● WATER
● OTHER

● SALT ● WATER
● OTHER

Another example of a large saltwater lake is the Dead Sea in the **MIDDLE EAST**. The Dead Sea is much saltier than water in the open ocean. In fact, it's so salty that no fish or plants can survive in the water – that's why it's called the 'Dead' Sea!

Salinity is a word that describes how salty water is. These pie charts show that water in the Dead Sea has a higher salinity than seawater.

ICE CAPS

Some oceans and seas get so cold that they freeze over to create giant ice sheets or ice packs. The Arctic Ocean surrounds the **NORTH POLE** and is so cold that some of the water is almost always frozen in a huge ice pack. This ice never completely melts, but it does shrink in the summer. It grows again in the winter as the melted ice freezes back over. However, as the world gets warmer every year, more and more of the Arctic ice pack is melting. In fact, the Arctic sea ice is melting so quickly that scientists are worried that it may never fully recover.

There is a positive correlation between time and Earth's temperature, but a negative correlation between time and the amount of Arctic sea ice remaining.

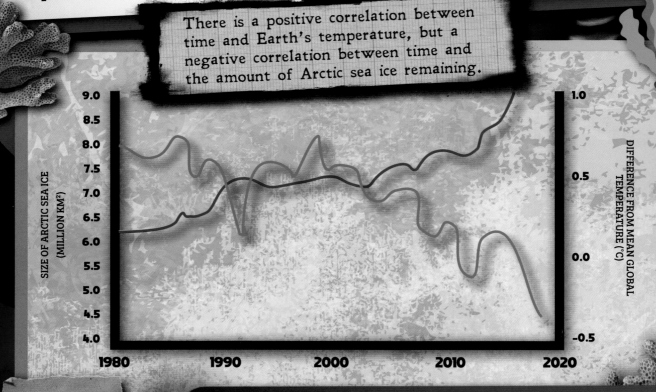

KEY:

ARCTIC SEA ICE

TEMPERATURE

This line graph shows clearly how the amount of sea ice in the Arctic is decreasing as Earth's temperature is increasing. Earth is now almost 1°C warmer than the **MEAN** temperature was between 1951 and 1980. As ice in the Arctic melts, animals like the polar bear and walrus are losing more of their habitat.

Antarctica is a continent covered in ice at the bottom of the Earth. It is made up of the land around the **SOUTH POLE** and is surrounded by the Southern Ocean. Just like the Arctic Ocean, parts of the Southern Ocean freeze over in winter to form ice sheets. The Antarctic ice sheet that covers the Antarctic continent is the largest ice sheet on Earth. It holds around 90% of all the freshwater on our planet and if it melted, it would raise the world's sea levels by up to 60 metres! It's normal for water to freeze and for ice to melt throughout the year, but it's important that they do so at the same **RATE** so that sea levels stay constant.

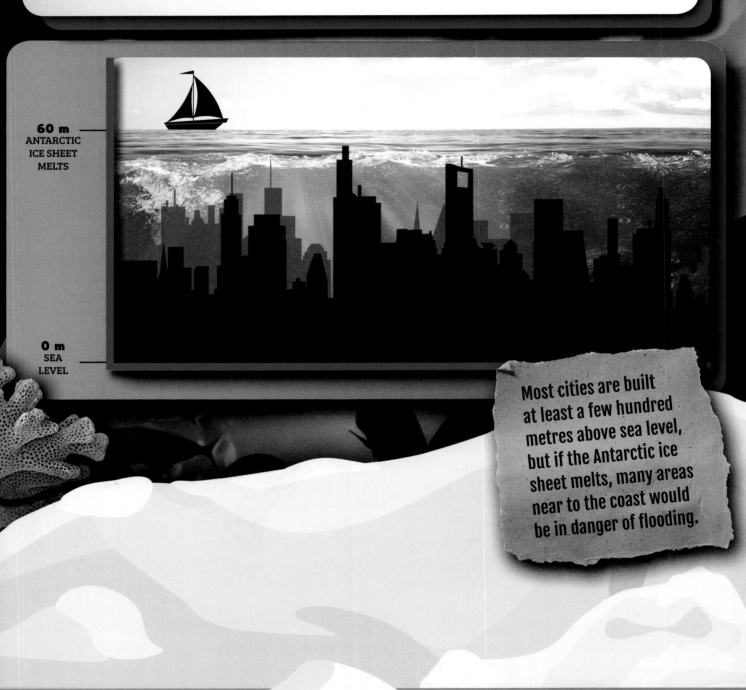

60 m
ANTARCTIC
ICE SHEET
MELTS

0 m
SEA
LEVEL

Most cities are built at least a few hundred metres above sea level, but if the Antarctic ice sheet melts, many areas near to the coast would be in danger of flooding.

THE WATER CYCLE

When snow and ice melts, it enters rivers and streams as part of the water cycle. The water cycle is how Earth's water is constantly moving and it's very important for all life on the planet.

The water cycle begins with the Sun heating the water on Earth and making it **EVAPORATE** and change to water vapour. It rises into the **ATMOSPHERE**, cools down and **CONDENSES** to become clouds. Winds blow the clouds around the world and the water falls back to Earth as rain or snow. Rain, snow and melted ice travel down from mountains and hills into rivers and streams, and eventually back into the ocean. The cycle begins again with the Sun warming and evaporating water on the surface of the ocean.

Some water seeps into the soil and trickles farther down underground through the earth. This water is called groundwater.

Water on Earth is constantly being recycled through the water cycle. No new water is created, and it can't be destroyed either. Instead, it moves through the cycle, changing between water vapour, liquid water, and ice.

RESERVOIR	AVERAGE RESIDENCE TIME
ANTARCTICA	20,000 YEARS
OCEANS	3,200 YEARS
GLACIERS	20 TO 100 YEARS
SEASONAL SNOW COVER	2 TO 6 MONTHS
SOIL MOISTURE	1 TO 2 MONTHS
GROUNDWATER (SHALLOW)	100 TO 200 YEARS
GROUNDWATER (DEEP)	10,000 YEARS
LAKES	50 TO 100 YEARS
RIVERS	2 TO 6 MONTHS
ATMOSPHERE	9 DAYS

Although water is always moving through the water cycle, it might be stored in some places for a longer time than it is in others. This is called the residence time and each place that the water is stored in is called a reservoir. In some reservoirs, like the frozen ice sheet in Antarctica, water could remain there for thousands of years, but in others it might only stay there for a few months before it moves on.

Around 496,000 CUBIC KILOMETRES of water evaporates from land and the ocean surface every year. This water stays in the atmosphere as clouds for around nine days before returning to Earth as snow or rain.

MARINE HABITATS

Habitats are the natural surroundings that a plant or animal lives in and they contain everything that the living thing needs to survive. Habitats can be found all over the world, even in the ocean – these are called marine habitats. Coral reefs are one example of a marine habitat. The largest coral reef in the world is the Great Barrier Reef off the north-eastern coast of Australia in the Pacific Ocean.

GREAT BARRIER REEF

The Great Barrier Reef is located in the Coral Sea and is actually made up of over 2,000 smaller reefs. The reefs stretch for over 2,000 km along the coast of Australia and take up an area of around 350,000 square km – that's around the same size as Germany!

The Great Barrier Reef is so big that it can be seen from space!

This bar chart makes it easy to compare the size of the Great Barrier Reef with countries from around the world.

Millions of tiny animals called polyps have created the Great Barrier Reef over millions of years. The polyps make themselves hard skeletons out of **MINERALS**. After the polyps die, the skeletons remain on the reef. More and more polyps build their skeletons on top of these old skeletons until eventually a huge coral reef is made! These can be used as homes for other animals and plants that help the reef grow even more.

The Great Barrier Reef is one of the most **BIODIVERSE** places on Earth and is home to thousands of different **SPECIES** of animals. 215 species of birds, 30 species of whales, dolphins and porpoises, 14 species of sea snakes and 6 species of sea turtles, as well as many other animals, all live in and around the Great Barrier Reef.

WHERE DO THE WORLD'S FISH SPECIES LIVE?

10% of all known species of fish on Earth can be found in the Great Barrier Reef.

10%

90%

● GREAT BARRIER REEF
● REST OF THE WORLD

THE COAST

A coast is the point where the edge of the land meets an ocean or sea. All coasts have features that make them different. Some coasts have caves and cliffs, and others might have beaches, dunes and mudflats.

The ocean shapes the coast and can completely change how an area looks. Sometimes, the sea can wear away parts of the land until it crumbles into the water below. This is called coastal erosion. **WEATHERING** and erosion can wear away coastal cliffs so much that, over many years, it can create caves. Cliffs along the southern coast of the UK are now eroding at a much faster rate than previous years. Up until around 150 years ago, these cliffs were eroding at a rate of around 2–6 centimetres (cm) a year and had been for about 7,000 years. However, over the past 150 years the rate has been much higher at around 22–32 cm a year.

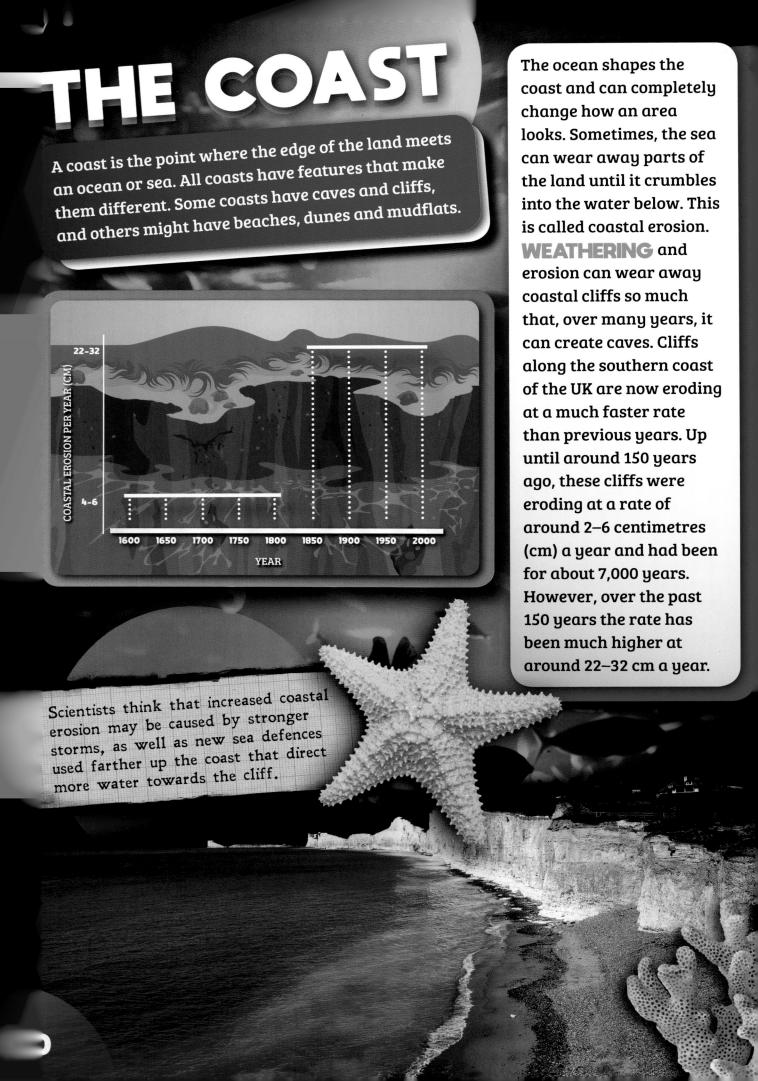

COASTAL EROSION PER YEAR (CM)

22–32

4–6

1600 1650 1700 1750 1800 1850 1900 1950 2000

YEAR

Scientists think that increased coastal erosion may be caused by stronger storms, as well as new sea defences used farther up the coast that direct more water towards the cliff.

BEACHES

Rocks and stones that fall into the sea are worn down by waves. Over many years, they're broken down into shingle – which is made up of tiny pebbles – and then eventually sand. The waves carry the shingle and sand to calm, shallow coastlines where they form beaches. Some beaches are sandy, and some are stony; some have lots of waves and some are very calm and still. Some people travel hundreds or even thousands of kilometres across the world to go on holiday to a specific beach. Australia, the US, and Spain are full of many beautiful, sandy beaches that are packed with TOURISTS during the summer.

LONGEST BEACHES

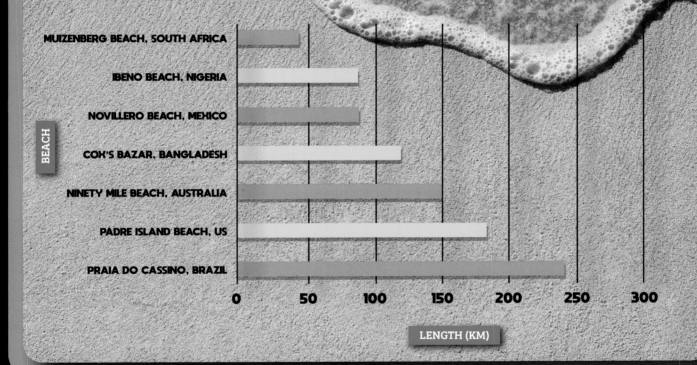

The longest beach in the world is thought to be Praia do Cassino beach in Brazil. Its long, sandy shores stretch for around 240 km along the south-eastern coast of Brazil. People travel here to sunbathe, play in the sea, and surf.

TIDES

In most places, the sea gets closer to and farther away from the coast four times a day. These changes are called tides. When the sea comes up the beach and the water level rises, it's called high tide. When the sea goes farther out and the water level falls again, it's called low tide.

The tides are controlled by the Moon's gravity which pulls on the Earth. Gravity is a pulling force that pulls objects in space towards each other. Gravity pulls Earth's oceans towards the Moon which creates something called a tidal bulge. This causes the sea level on Earth to rise on the side that is facing the Moon, which causes the high tide.

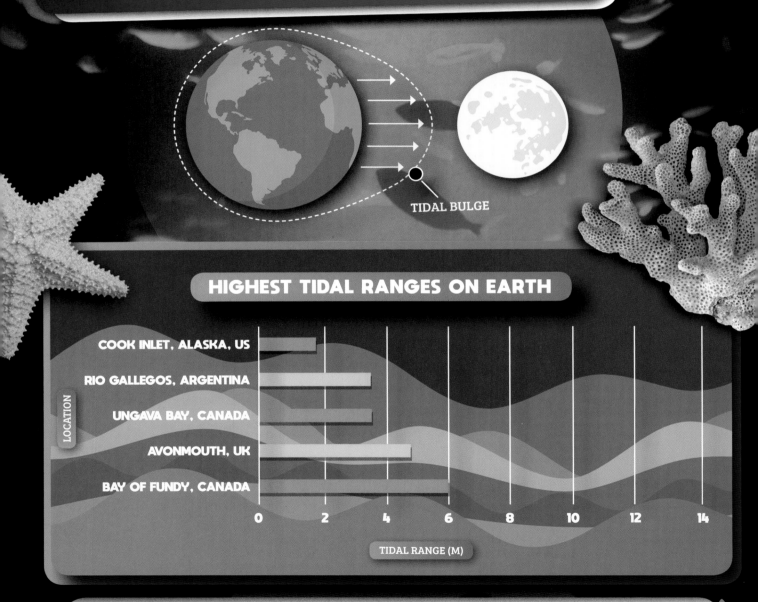

TIDAL BULGE

HIGHEST TIDAL RANGES ON EARTH

LOCATION

COOK INLET, ALASKA, US

RIO GALLEGOS, ARGENTINA

UNGAVA BAY, CANADA

AVONMOUTH, UK

BAY OF FUNDY, CANADA

0   2   4   6   8   10   12   14

TIDAL RANGE (M)

Tidal range is the difference in sea level between high tide and low tide. It can tell us how far the sea has travelled either in or out of the beach. The Bay of Fundy in Canada has the highest tidal range. There is around 11.7 metres difference between every high and low tide.

WAVES

Unlike tides, waves are caused by the wind, so they can crash into the coast hundreds or even thousands of times every day and all throughout the night. Some seas that have more wind will be choppier than others, but it's rare to have a sea that's completely calm. When powerful waves crash into coastlines and cliffs, the seawater enters cracks in the rock and forces the rock apart. This weakens and erodes the rock.

Some waves are small and only reach a few centimetres above the shore, but others can reach several metres high before they **BREAK**. These high, powerful waves can wear away cliffs, but they are also great for surfers who travel around different beaches looking for good waves to surf.

SURFER	LOCATION	WAVE HEIGHT (M)
MARK PARSONS	CORTES BANK, CALIFORNIA, US	21
PETE CABRINHA	JAWS, MAUI, HAWAII, US	21
CARLOS BURLE	MAVERICKS, CALIFORNIA, US	20
DAN MOORE	JAWS, MAUI, HAWAII, US	20
BRAD GERLACH	TODOS SANTOS, MEXICO	20
GARRETT MCNAMARA	PRAIA DO NORTE, NAZARE, PORTUGAL	23.7

This table and bar chart show some of the highest waves people have surfed. Garrett McNamara broke the world record for the largest wave surfed in 2011 when he surfed down a 23.7-metre-high wave off the coast of Portugal.

TSUNAMIS

Some waves are so high and so fast that they can wipe out entire towns and cities and destroy beaches in a matter of minutes. These waves are usually part of something called a tsunami. A tsunami is a series of huge, fast-moving waves that can travel at speeds of 700 kilometres per hour (kph) across the ocean and hit the coast at heights of up to 60 m.

Tsunamis aren't caused by the wind. These waves are usually triggered by an earthquake underneath the ocean floor that shakes the seabed and causes the water to **SURGE** upwards. While out in the open ocean, tsunami waves are usually still quite low. However, when they reach the shore, the water is a lot shallower, so they slow down in speed and grow in height.

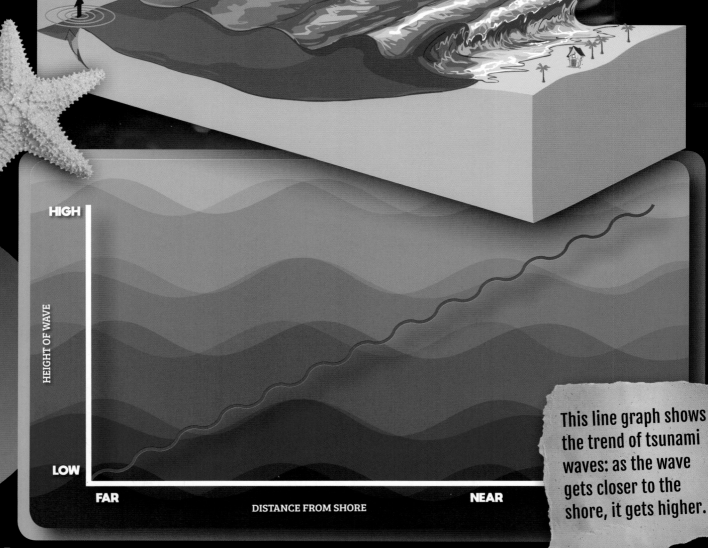

HEIGHT OF WAVE

HIGH

LOW

FAR

NEAR

DISTANCE FROM SHORE

This line graph shows the trend of tsunami waves: as the wave gets closer to the shore, it gets higher.

Tsunamis destroy coastal areas around the world every year, but some tsunami waves are a lot higher and a lot deadlier than others. The highest tsunami wave in recent history was the Lituya Bay tsunami in Alaska, 1958. Although the wave was over 500 m high, only five people were killed by the tsunami and the earthquake that triggered it.

HIGHEST TSUNAMI WAVES

WAVE HEIGHT (M)

600
500
400
300
200
100
0

JAPAN, 1896 | LITUYA BAY, ALASKA, 1958 | CHILE, 1960 | INDIAN OCEAN, 2004

TSUNAMI LOCATION

The deadliest tsunamis aren't always the highest. For example, the Indian Ocean tsunami in 2004 reached a height of around 30 m. This is over 10 times smaller than the Lituya Bay tsunami wave, but it killed around 220,000 people across Indonesia, Sri Lanka, India and Thailand. Many people consider the Indian Ocean tsunami to be the most DESTRUCTIVE tsunami in history.

The Indian Ocean tsunami is sometimes called the South Asian tsunami, the Indonesian tsunami, or the Boxing Day tsunami. It was triggered by one of the largest earthquakes ever recorded.

CURRENTS

Currents are the ways in which water constantly moves through the world's oceans. Currents move in a specific direction and follow a pattern. They are usually driven by winds, tides, and how **DENSE** the water is. Ocean currents can be split into two main groups: surface currents that occur at the top 100 metres of the ocean, and deep-sea currents that can be found 100 metres and deeper, below the ocean's surface. Currents can also be controlled by the Moon's gravity and the **ROTATION** of Earth.

Currents carry warm and cold water around the world. They can affect the weather and climate of countries that are found near to these currents. Warm ocean currents, like the Gulf Stream, make areas warmer while cold ocean currents, like the Humboldt, or Peru, Current make areas cooler.

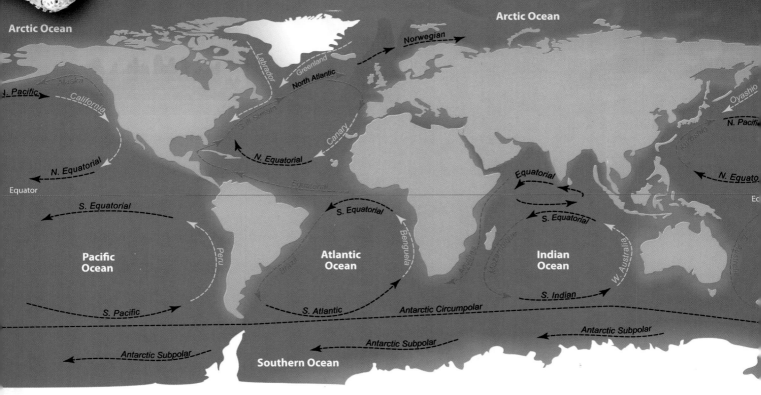

Arctic Ocean

Arctic Ocean

Norwegian

Labrador

Greenland

North Atlantic

Alaska

N. Pacific

California

Oyashio

N. Pacific

Gulf Stream

Canary

N. Equatorial

N. Equatorial

Kuroshio

N. Equatorial

N. Equatorial

Equator

Equatorial

Equatorial

S. Equatorial

S. Equatorial

S. Equatorial

S. Equatorial

Pacific
Ocean

Peru

Brazil

Atlantic
Ocean

Benguela

Agulhas

Mozambique

Indian
Ocean

W. Australia

Equator

S. Pacific

S. Atlantic

Antarctic Circumpolar

S. Indian

Antarctic Subpolar

Antarctic Subpolar

Antarctic Subpolar

Southern Ocean

- - - - -▶ WARM CURRENT   ──────▶ COLD CURRENT   - - - - -▶ NEUTRAL CURRENT

The Gulf Stream begins in the Gulf of Mexico. It transports warm seawater along the east coast of the US and across the Atlantic Ocean towards western Europe. The Gulf Stream gives people living in Florida, on the east coast of the US, warmer winters and cooler summers than the surrounding areas. It also keeps western Europe's climate warm and **TEMPERATE**. Scientists **ESTIMATE** that, without the Gulf Stream, the UK would be around 5°C cooler. Its climate would be similar to that of Calgary, Canada, which has temperatures of between around 0°C and -12°C during winter.

The Gulf Stream begins off the coast of eastern Mexico in the Gulf of Mexico. It's a warm ocean current.

The UK would be a lot cooler without the Gulf Stream. Temperatures in winter would struggle to reach above 2°C, and temperatures in summer would stay at around 14°C or below.

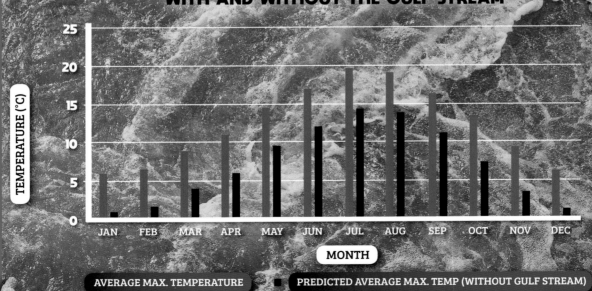

AVERAGE MONTHLY MAXIMUM TEMPERATURE IN THE UK WITH AND WITHOUT THE GULF STREAM

TEMPERATURE (°C)

25
20
15
10
5
0

JAN   FEB   MAR   APR   MAY   JUN   JUL   AUG   SEP   OCT   NOV   DEC

MONTH

AVERAGE MAX. TEMPERATURE   ■ PREDICTED AVERAGE MAX. TEMP (WITHOUT GULF STREAM)

PLASTIC IN OUR OCEANS
THE GREAT PACIFIC GARBAGE PATCH

Some ocean currents join to make up huge rotating circles called vortexes or gyres. There are five major ocean gyres on Earth and one of these is the North Pacific Subtropical Gyre. The Great Pacific Garbage Patch, or GPGP, is a huge collection of litter in the Pacific Ocean. The GPGP is made up of the Western Garbage Patch and the Eastern Garbage Patch. They're connected by the North Pacific Subtropical Gyre, which carries rubbish between the two patches until it eventually collects in the middle of the gyre. Most of the GPGP is made up of tiny bits of plastic, called microplastics. Although these microplastics can't be seen by the NAKED EYE, they're very harmful for animals living in the ocean.

Most rubbish in the GPGP comes from North America and Japan, while around 20% comes from boats, OFFSHORE OIL PLATFORMS, and cargo ships that dump or lose their CARGO into the sea.

20%

80%

● LAND-BASED RUBBISH

● OFFSHORE RUBBISH

Most plastics take hundreds of years to DECOMPOSE. They break down into smaller pieces that are eaten by fish and other animals. The plastics then release chemicals into the animals that have eaten them.

FRIENDLY FLOATEES

In 1992, over 28,000 plastic bath toys called Friendly Floatees fell from a cargo ship into the Pacific Ocean. Because these bath toys are made from plastic, they didn't break down in the water or sink to the bottom of the ocean. Instead, they floated on the surface and were transported across the world's oceans by currents. Since 1992, the Friendly Floatees have been washing up on coasts all around the world.

OCEANOGRAPHERS such as Curtis Ebbesmeyer have been tracking the Friendly Floatees' journeys since 1992. They've been found all over the world in places such as Alaska, Japan, Hawaii, Australia and Scotland. They've taught scientists and oceanographers a lot about surface currents, gyres, and garbage patches. Although many of the Friendly Floatees have now been found, thousands are still at sea. In fact, there are still around 2,000 floating in the North Pacific Subtropical Gyre.

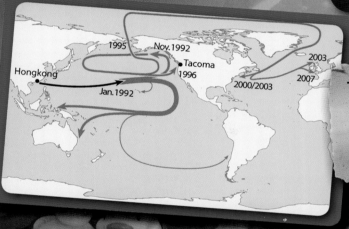

This map shows the journeys taken by some of the Friendly Floatees.

ACTIVITY: GET SMART!

Do you live near a beach? Maybe you could go there with an adult. Record how many people you see at the beach at different times throughout the day. Put all of your results into a frequency table and use this to make a line graph. At what time of the day is the beach busiest? When is it quietest?

TIME	NUMBER OF PEOPLE	TOTAL
9:00	| | |	3
10:00	| | | |	4
11:00	卌 |	6
12:00	卌 卌	10
13:00	卌 卌 | | |	13
14:00	卌 卌 | |	12
15:00	卌 卌	10
16:00	卌 | |	7
17:00	| | | |	4

HOW MANY PEOPLE CAME TO THE BEACH TODAY?

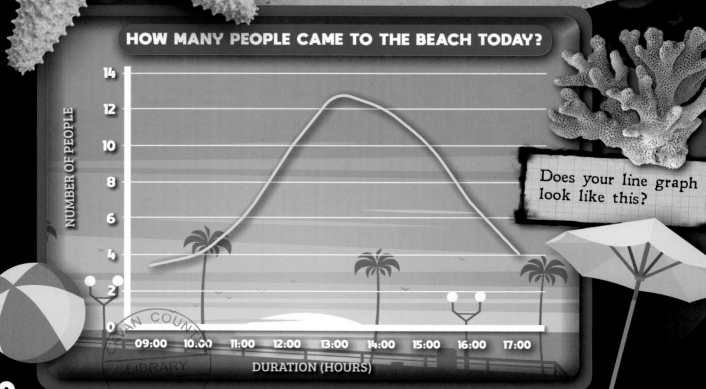

Does your line graph look like this?

GLOSSARY

ATMOSPHERE	the mixture of gases that make up the air and surround the Earth
BIODIVERSE	when an area has lots of different types of animals or plants
BREAK	when a wave curls over and turns to white foam
CARGO	items carried on ships, including cattle, food, tools and furniture
CLIMATE	the common weather in a certain place
CONDENSES	changes from a gas or vapour into a liquid
CONSTANT	unending or never changing
CONTINENTS	very large areas of land that are made up of many countries, like Africa and Europe
CRUST	the hard outermost layer of the Earth
CUBIC KILOMETRES	a measurement of an area that is a cube with each side being a kilometre in length
DECOMPOSE	decay or rot
DENSE	tightly packed
DESTRUCTIVE	to destroy or cause destruction
EQUATOR	the imaginary line around the Earth that is an equal distance from the North and South Poles
ESTIMATE	guess based on facts
EVAPORATE	turn from a liquid into a gas or vapour, usually through heat
GLACIERS	large masses of ice that move very slowly
HABITATS	the natural environments in which animals or plants live
INTERPRET	to understand or work out
LANDLOCKED	completely surrounded by land with no access to the sea
MANNED	controlled or performed by a human
MEAN	the middle value or point between two extremes
MIDDLE EAST	an area of western Asia that lies between Asia and Africa
MINERALS	natural, useful and sometimes valuable substances, often obtained from rocks in the ground
NAKED EYE	used to describe sight that is unaided by glasses, binoculars or telescopes
NORTH POLE	the most northern point on Earth
OCEANOGRAPHERS	scientists that study the oceans
OFFSHORE OIL PLATFORMS	large structures out in the sea that drill deep into the ground to find oil
PEAK	the pointy top of a hill or mountain
POSITIVE CORRELATION	a relationship between two sets of data where they increase or decrease together
RATE	how often something happens
ROTATION	the action of spinning around a central point
SEA LEVEL	the level of the sea's surface
SHORES	the land along the edge of the sea
SOUTH POLE	the most southern point on Earth
SPECIES	a group of very similar animals or plants that are capable of producing young together
SQUARE KILOMETRES	a measurement of an area that is a square with each side being a kilometre in length
SURGE	a sudden and very strong increase
TEMPERATE	a region or climate that is characterised by mild temperatures
TOURISTS	people who are visiting a place for pleasure
WEATHERING	the effect that wind, rain, and other weather conditions have on breaking down or wearing away rocks

INDEX